A Wandering Guidebook:

St. Louis, MO – Forest Park & Central West End

Tom Alyea

Copyright © 2015 Tom Alyea

All rights reserved.

ISBN-13: 978-1517038007

ISBN-10: 1517038006

St. Louis, MO – Forest Park and Central West End

A Wandering Walk Guide Book

CONTENTS

	Acknowledgments	i
1	Map of Walking Tour	2
2	Walking Tour	4
	Stop 1 – Dennis and Judith Jones Visitor Center	8
	Stop 2 – Missouri History Museum	9
	Stop 3 – Cabanne House	10
	Stop 4 – Max Steinberg Skating Rink	11
	Stop 5 – McDonnell Planetarium	12
	Stop 6 – St. Louis Science Center	13
	Stop 7 – St. Louis Zoo	14
	Stop 8 – World's Fair Pavilion	16
	Stop 9 – Saint Louis Art Museum	17
	Stop 10 – The Grand Basin	18
	Stop 11 – Washington University	19
	Stop 12 – Lindell Blvd. Mansions and Route 66	22
	Stop 13 – Pagoda Circle Bandstand	24
	Stop 14 – Municipal Theater	25
	Stop 15 – The Jewel Box	26
	Stop 16 – Victorian Footbridge	27

- Stop 17 – Central West End Neighborhood 28
- Stop 18 – Forest Park Hotel 30
- Stop 19 – Butler House 31
- Stop 20 – Cathedral Basilica of St. Louis 32
- Stop 21 – Fullerton's Westminster Place 34
- Stop 22 – Second Presbyterian Church 35
- Stop 23 – Joseph Erlanger House 36

3 Other Sites to Visit in the Region 38

NOTES

Every attempt has been made to ensure that the information in this walk guide is accurate and the route is safe. The author assumes no responsibility for injury while walking. Also, you may experience construction or other obstacles on your journey. The map provided should be used in those cases.

1
WALKING TOUR MAP

A Wandering Walk Guide Book

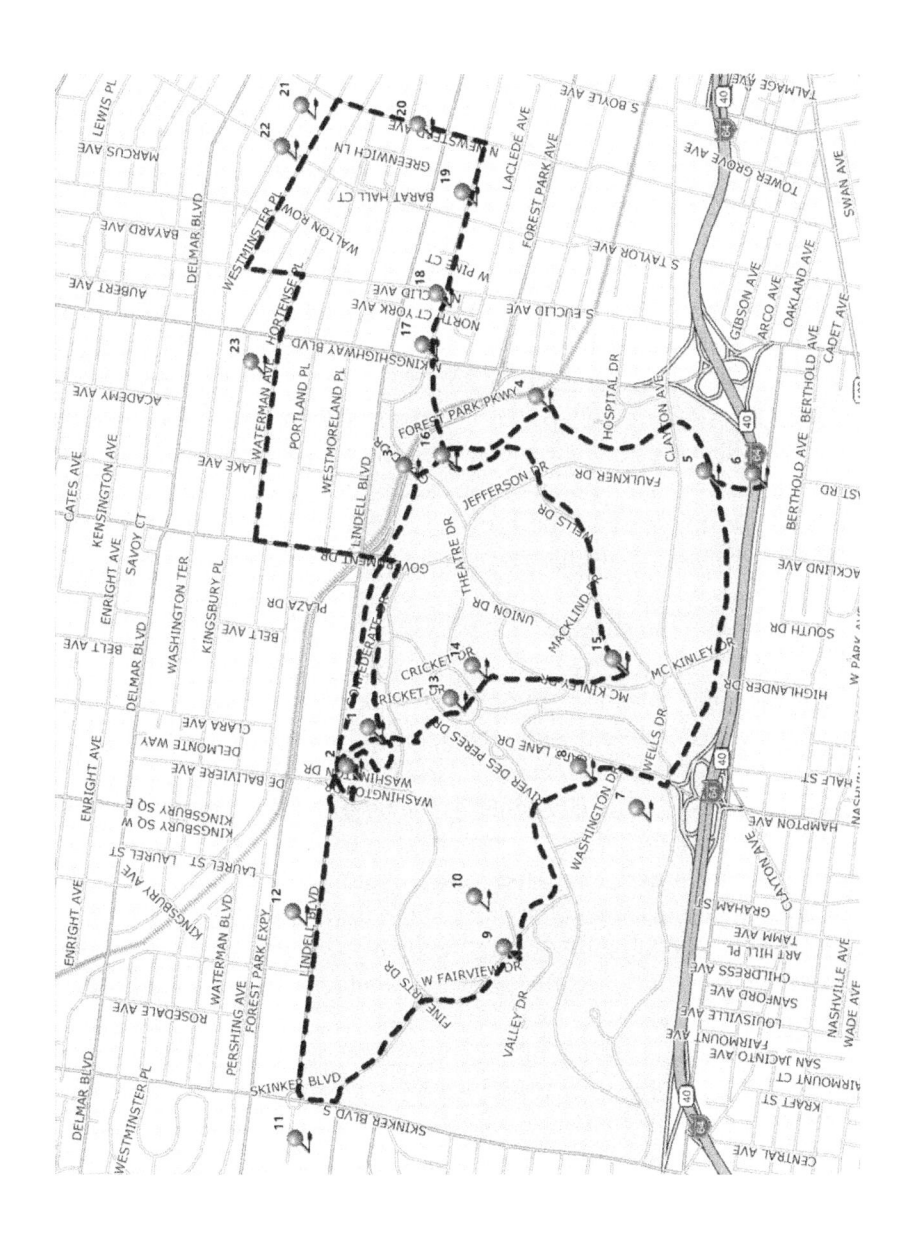

2
WALKING TOUR

Welcome to Forest Park and the Central West End District of St. Louis. You are about to embark on a 10-mile walking tour throughout an area known as the "heart of St. Louis." Forest Park is one of the largest public parks in the nation and was the site of the 1904 St. Louis World's Fair. Inside this oasis within the city of St. Louis, you will find a variety of attractions, including the St. Louis Zoo, the Saint Louis Art Museum, the Missouri History Museum, and The Muny outdoor theater. This walk will take you by all these sites, and more. The walking route will extend beyond Forest Park so you can experience the historic district known as the Central West End. On this part of the tour you, will visit the beautiful St. Louis Basilica and historic mansions that sit on their own private streets.

Forest Park – the Origins

The plans and development of Forest Park date back as far as 1872. A prominent St. Louis developer by the name of Hiram Leffingwell proposed that a 1,300-acre park be created on land he owned that was about three miles west of the St. Louis city limits. At the time, the area before you today was heavily forested and was the perfect spot for a new city park that would rival the largest city parks in the nation. Throughout 1872-1874 there were legal challenges that delayed the development of the land into a park. In 1875, the Missouri General Assembly was able to pass the Forest Park Act, which established the park and created a county-wide property tax to fund it.

It's hard to imagine today, but as you stand looking out at tall buildings, super highways, and thousands of people, this entire area was once in the 'rural' portion of the city and all the roads were unpaved. Running diagonally across the parkland was the River des Peres. During the dry season, the river was hardly noticed, but during the rainy months, the river flooded and created a swampy mess of tangled trees and vegetation. The first step in developing the park was to start taming the land.

The job of transforming the rural, wooded land into a park was directed by designers Maximillian Kern and Julius Pitzman. They carved paths and trails through the woodlands, erected a large music stand, and did what they could to control the troublesome River des Peres. Their efforts were rewarded when the park was officially dedicated on June 24, 1876. A crowd of 50,000 made their way from the city to view the city's newest park. By the late 1800's, streetcars were reaching the park. Prior to the turn of the 20th century, nearly 3 million visitors a year were coming to Forest Park to enjoy the peace and quiet of nature as they escaped from the hustle and bustle of life in the city not three miles away.

The 1904 St. Louis World's Fair

In 1901, St. Louis was selected as the location for the Louisiana Purchase Exposition to be held in 1904. This event, commonly called the St. Louis World's Fair, would transform the park into what you see today. Along with the Fair, St. Louis was also host to the 1904 Summer Olympic games. Most of the fifteen competitive sporting events were held on the grounds of Washington University, which is west of Forest Park. Diving, swimming, and water polo events were held on the grounds of Forest Park.

Landscape designer George Kessler transformed Forest Park in preparation for the 1904 World's Fair. It's hard to imagine, but during the year-long celebration visitors had the chance to walk by nearly 1,500 buildings that were connected by over 75 miles of new roads and walkways. One building, the Palace of Agricultural, was reported to cover over 20 acres. 62 foreign nations erected exhibition halls to showcase the commercial and cultural aspects of their countries. In 1904, there were 45 states in the U.S. and 43 of those states had a building or some structure to highlight the state at the Fair. There were also exhibits and buildings constructed by industries, cities, private organizations, and corporations. Not to mention theater groups and music schools. A world's fair would not be complete without exciting rides. Over 50 types of amusements rides could be found on the grounds at any time.

It was estimated that well over 19 million people traveled to St. Louis in 1904 to enjoy the World's Fair. It's easy to see why the most popular song in America during that time was *Meet Me in St. Louis, Louis*. Some of the more notable attendees and participants of the fair include:

>John Philip Sousa. Sousa conducted his band on Opening Day and on many days throughout the fair. As Sousa directed the band into a rousing patriotic song, President Theodore Roosevelt opened the Fair via telegraph. Roosevelt was running

for President at the time and felt it would be improper for him to attend in person.

Scott Joplin. Ragtime music was becoming very popular during the early 1900's. One of the most famous of the Ragtime composers was local St. Louis composer Scott Joplin. Joplin wrote one of his masterpieces, *The Cascades,* specifically for the Fair. He said the waterfalls of the Grand Basin were his inspiration

Geronimo. The former war chief of the Apache Nation was "on display" in a teepee. He is reported to have made quite a bit of money signing autographs.

Jack Daniel. Daniel was an emerging distiller from Tennessee who entered his whiskey into the World's Fair whiskey competition. It took four hours of deliberation, and constant sampling of his product by the judges, to award him the Gold Medal for the finest whiskey in the world.

Many new types of food were either invented or popularized at the fair. These include the waffle-style ice cream cone, hamburgers, hot dogs, peanut butter, iced tea, and cotton candy. The soft drink, Dr. Pepper, and the cereal, Puffed Wheat, were also introduced at the fair.

Forest Park after the World's Fair

The fair's landscape architect, George Kessler, dramatically changed the park for the Fair. His design and the impact he made are seen today. The wetlands areas on the western portion of the park were drained to create several waterfalls and five connected lagoons. The River des Peres was diverted underground to avoid the sanitary issues that swampy waters created throughout the park. During Kessler's days, wooden boxes were used to divert the water. In the 1930's, huge concrete pipes were installed underground to allow the river to flow. The river remains underground in the park today. Thousands of trees and new vistas were created that continue to flourish and make the park an oasis of nature surrounded by the noise of big city life.

The World's Fair generated a large profit for the city of St. Louis. This allowed the directors of the Fair to donate several of the buildings to the city as permanent monuments. While nearly all of the 1,500 buildings that were constructed during the Fair were razed soon after the Fair ended, several remain today. These include the Missouri History Museum, which the fair's directors donated as a monument to Thomas Jefferson. Other structures surviving from the days of the St. Louis World's Fair that you will see on your tour include the Saint Louis Art Museum, the Grand Basis, the Apotheosis of St. Louis (a statue of French King Louis IX), and the 1904 Bird Cage (now a part of the St. Louis Zoo).

The Central West End Historic District

The Central West End is an affluent neighborhood that borders much of Forest Park. During this part of the walking tour, you will see many of the mansions and other fine homes that were constructed for the wealthy of St. Louis at the turn of the 20th century. This neighborhood is also the site of the Cathedral Basilica of St. Louis.

The commercial area of the Central West End is mainly along Euclid Avenue. Here you will find dozens of local restaurants and shops. Turn of the 20th century lamp posts and cobblestone remain today. Unique to the Central West End are the private streets where the historic homes face. Some of the finest 20th century "streetscapes" in the United States can be found within the Central West End. These park-like streets offer beautiful flowers and tree-shaded streets to stroll.

The Central West End was home to Playwright Tennessee Williams and poet T.S. Eliot.

It's time to tighten those shoelaces and grab your water bottle and let your tour of Forest Park and the Central West End begin...

> **Start your walking tour by standing in front of the Dennis and Judith Jones Visitor and Education Center and facing the parking lot area.**

Stop 1:
Dennis and Judith Jones Visitor and Education Center
(5595 Grand Drive)

Your walking tour will begin at the historic Dennis and Judith Jones Visitor and Education Center in Forest Park. This building was originally constructed in 1892 as a streetcar station for the Lindell Railway. The Spanish Revival style building was used during the 1904 World's Fair. After the Fair, the building became a golf shop and locker room for those headed to the links on the Forest Park Golf Course.

In the early 2000's, the building was renovated and converted into the Forest Park Visitor Center. Part of the restoration included the clock tower, which has operated since the building was originally constructed. Inside the Visitor's Center you will find restrooms, a small café, and information and exhibits about Forest Park. The volunteers for the Missouri Department of Conservation can help you with anything you need to enjoy the park.

> Take the sidewalk on the right and start walking towards the tennis courts.
> Turn RIGHT on the paved walking trail just before Grand St.
> Turn LEFT at the first intersection on the paved trail. You will be heading towards Lindell Blvd.
> Continue on the trail as you come to Stop 2.

Stop 2: Missouri History Museum (5700 Lindell Blvd.)

Of the 1,500 buildings that were erected as part of the 1904 St. Louis World's Fair, only a handful of those buildings exist today. The Missouri History Museum is one of those. The older parts of the original building were used as the main entrance to the World's Fair.

Using profits from the Fair, the building was renovated in 1913 as the first national monument to Thomas Jefferson. Inside, is a 16-ton statue of Thomas Jefferson that was sculpted by noted artist Karl Bitter.

Exhibits in the museum tell the story of the history of Missouri, St. Louis, and the 1904 World's Fair. A large number of artifacts from the Lewis and Clark Expedition are also on display in the museum. Hanging proudly in the front atrium is a replica of Charles Lindbergh's *"The Spirit of St. Louis"* airplane. This plane was used in the 1957 film that starred Jimmy Stewart who portrayed this hometown hero on his Trans-Atlantic flight to Europe.

St. Louis, MO – Forest Park and Central West End

> - Continue past the front entrance of the museum and turn RIGHT at the stop light at Lindell Blvd.
> - Turn Right again and continue on the trail with Lindell Blvd. on your left and the museum on your right.
> - After crossing the next stoplight, continue straight on the OUTER walking trail.
> - Cross Cricket Drive and continue straight on walking trail to Stop 3

Stop 3: Cabanne House (5300 Lindell Blvd.)

Born in 1773 in France, Jean Pierre Cabanne moved to St. Louis in 1796 as one of the founders of the American Fur Company and the Bank of St. Louis. In 1819, he built what is considered to be the first brick farmhouse west of the Mississippi River. In 1875, the Cabanne family sold the land to the city as part of the creation of Forest Park. The original farmhouse was converted into a lodge, but later demolished in the 1880's.

The current Cabanne House was built in the late 1880's. The Second Empire style home served as the Forest Park Superintendent's home until 1966 when a fire damaged much of the building. In the 1980's, the home was renovated and is used as a park volunteer office building and for special events.

> Continue on walking trail and cross the intersection at Union Dr. Continue on paved walking trail.
> Cross the intersection at Grand Dr. and continue on walking trail to Stop 4.

Stop 4:
Max Steinberg Skating Rink
(400 Jefferson Dr.)

In 1957, the Steinberg Charitable Trust donated $600,000 for the construction of one of the largest outdoor ice skating rinks in the Midwest. The rink is open for ice skating throughout the cold, winter months of Forest Park. During the 1950's and 1960's, the rink was the site of several amateur ice hockey teams that played on a regular basis throughout the winter. Surprisingly, the rink was too large for a regulation hockey game and most teams moved to indoor facilities in the later part of the 20th century.

In the early 2000's, the rink was renovated at cost of $1.4 million. A new rink surface, a modern ice-making system, and lights were added. The Snowflake Café also received an extensive makeover. To enhance the beauty of this part of Forest Park during the summer months, a prairie and wetlands area, with gravel walking paths and birdwatching sites, were added as part of the renovation.

> Continue on paved walking trail.
> Cross Clayton Ave intersection and continue on the trail, and up the hill, to Stop 5.

Stop 5:
McDonnell Planetarium
(5050 Oakland Ave.)

In 1955, the voters of the city of St. Louis approved a major bond issue. $1 million of that bond was designated to be used to build a new planetarium in the city. This was in the early years of the Space Race, and public interest was high in all things related to space and space travel. It took an additional eight years to locate a spot for the planetarium and to raise more money for the construction of the building. James McDonnell, founder of St. Louis based McDonnell Aircraft Corporation, provided much of the additional funds to complete the building. In his honor, the planetarium was named the James S. McDonnell Planetarium when the building was dedicate in May 1963.

The Planetarium was designed by Gyo Obata with a very unique shape. Architectural Forum Magazine once described it as, "looking like some strange craft spun down to earth from outer space." A tradition, that began as a prank, during the holiday season is for the Planetarium's unique building to be wrapped in a gigantic holiday ribbon and bow.

> **Look to your left for Stop 6.**

Stop 6:
St. Louis Science Center
(5050 Oakland Ave.)

The St. Louis Science Center is connected to Forest Park by a pedestrian walkway over Oakland Avenue and I-64. The Science Center is among one of the largest of its kind in the United States. With 300,000 square feet of space and over 750 exhibits, the Science Center is consistently ranked as one of the top 5 science centers of its kind in the U.S. The McDonnell Planetarium is part of the entire Science Center complex. Across the walkway, you will find several large exhibition buildings, an Omnimax© theater, and an air-supported building called the Exploradome©.

Inside the Science Center are exhibits devoted to Earth science, emerging technologies, life sciences, physical sciences, and chemistry. Special exhibits are held throughout the year. The most popular exhibition to date was when the Science Center hosted *Star Trek: The Exhibition.* In 2012, this showcase attracted millions of visitors as they viewed props, costumes, and other artifacts from the popular TV show. The exhibitions most popular attraction was the full-size replica of the bridge from the USS Enterprise.

St. Louis, MO – Forest Park and Central West End

> ➤ **Continue on walking trail.**
> ➤ **Go under the tunnel at Hampton Ave.**
> ➤ **About 50' after exiting the tunnel, turn RIGHT on sidewalk to the roundabout.**
> ➤ **Left at the pedestrian crossing at the roundabout.**
> ➤ **Right on the sidewalk to the animal sculpture and Stop 7.**

Stop 7:
St. Louis Zoo
(1 Government Dr.)

By far, the most visited attraction in Forest Park is the St. Louis Zoo. This zoo, which remains free of admission, opened in 1910. It is one of the largest and most popular zoos in the nation. 3 million visitors come to the zoo each year to view the more than 18,000 animals throughout the park. Inside are five animal zones where you can see elephants, lions, penguins, polar bears, tigers, apes, and monkeys. Two buildings that date back to the 1904 St. Louis World's Fair can be found inside the zoo. The free-standing Flight Cage features exotic birds from around the world. The herpetarium still retains the glamour of the building that was completed to showcase snakes and reptiles.

The St. Louis Zoological Park, as it is correctly named, is one of the leading zoos in the nation for animal management, research, conservation, and education. One of the largest animal nurseries in the nation can be found on the grounds of the zoo.

The zoo had its beginnings as part of the 1904 World's Fair. The Smithsonian Institution in Washington, DC, constructed the world's largest walk-through bird cage for the Fair. The citizens of St. Louis were so enamored of this exhibit that they purchased the Flight Cage for $3,500 rather than have it dismantled and shipped back to DC. This would become the first exhibition of the new zoo that the citizens were looking to build.

By the 1920's, public interest in zoos around the world was at an all-time high. The St. Louis Zoo benefited from this popularity and was quickly able to raise money to construct new Bear Pits, a Primate House, and a new Reptile House. As the nation worked its way through the Great Depression during the 1930's, the Antelope House and the Ape House were constructed with funds from the Civil Works Administration program created by President Franklin D. Roosevelt. Many people think that exhibiting pandas are a modern-age phenomenon in zoos. But that is not true in the case of the St. Louis Zoo. In 1939, the zoo was able to acquire Happy and Pao Pei from the Chinese government. Happy dies in 1945 and Pao Pei lived until 1954.

Construction of new exhibits is constant at the St. Louis Zoo. One of the most famous directors of the zoo was able to lead a huge construction boom during the 1960's and 1970's. Marlin Perkins used his fame as host of the *Mutual of Omaha's Wild Kingdom* TV show to attract donors to support the construction of major new exhibits. The Big Cat Country area and the Jungle of the Apes exhibition space are a direct result of Marlin's fund-raising efforts.

In the late 20th century, the zoo saw additional exhibits and educational space created. A two-story classroom and reference library were added along with new offices and restaurants.

Since 2000, the Zoo has added an insectarium, butterfly house, a penguin house, and, most recently, a new polar bear area.

> **Continue straight on sidewalk with Zoo on your left and Hampton Ave. on your right.**
> **Cross Washington Dr. and continue straight on sidewalk to Stop 8.**

Stop 8:
World's Fair Pavilion
(Government Hill)

While the name on this building is called the World's Fair Pavilion, it was never a part of the 1904 World's Fair held on the grounds of Forest Park. This large picnic and events pavilion was constructed in 1910 as a gift from the Louisiana Purchase Exposition Committee. The committee had made promises to restore and beautify Forest Park after the World's Fair ended. This building was a gift to the residents of St. Louis as a "thank you" for their hard work and generosity in helping to hold a successful World's Fair.

In early 2000, the building received a $1.1 million restoration effort. New restrooms and a catering kitchen were added along with new lighting. The twin towers of the structure were also reconstructed. Today, the pavilion is a popular location for weddings, large corporate events, or just a place to hang out and watch the fountains on the grounds below.

> Walk through the Pavilion and down the steps to view the fountain.
> Turn Right, then left, to walk down to the fountain.
> Cross Government and turn LEFT on walking trail.
> At the intersection at Washington Dr., turn RIGHT on walking trail.
> Turn Left at "Y" on walking trail up the hill toward the Art Museum.
> Turn RIGHT at the sidewalk at Fine Arts Dr. to Stop 9.

Stop 9: Saint Louis Art Museum (One Fine Arts Dr.)

The building that today houses the Saint Louis Art Museum was initially called the Palace of Fine Arts during the St. Louis World's Fair in 1904. It was also the building the electricity industry used to showcase two new inventions – the electrical plug and wall outlet. The museum traces its origins back to the Saint Louis School and Museum of Fine Arts that was founded in 1881 on the campus of Washington University near Forest Park.

Inside are world famous paintings, sculptures, and cultural objects from around the world. Admission to the museum is free.

> **Walk past the statue of St. Louis, and look out on the Forest Park grounds to Stop 10.**

Stop 10: The Grand Basin (Forest Park)

As you gaze out at the Forest Park Grand Basin, you are being treated to a glimpse of what the area looked like during the glory days of the 1904 World's Fair. The Grand Basin was designed to showcase the finest water features and fountains of the early 20th century. It's easy to imagine men in bowler hats and women with parasols strolling along the Grand Basin as they enjoyed a day at the World's Fair. With a magnificent view up to the Saint Louis Art Museum, the grounds have become a popular location for weddings and summer concerts.

In the center of the Grand Basin are two large architectural fountains that feature jets that propel water up to 50 feet in the sky. Artistic spray rings surround each of the fountains. The fountains proved a show of their own and offer a cool, relaxing spot to rest during the warm days of summer in St. Louis.

> Continue on sidewalk past the Art Museum and walk down the hill.
> Turn LEFT on Lagoon Dr.
> Cross Skinker Blvd., and turn RIGHT on sidewalk.
> Continue on sidewalk to the stoplight at Lindell Blvd.
> Pause here for Stop 11.
> *(Note, if you would like to visit Washington University and Francis Field, site of the 1904 Olympics, turn left into the Washington University Campus and walk approximately 1.5 miles through campus to the far end where Francis Field can be found. Return back to this point if you choose this option.)*

Stop 11: Washington University and the 1904 Summer Olympics (One Brookings Dr.)

Washington University

Washington University in St. Louis, commonly called WashU, is a private university that was founded in 1853. The university was named after George Washington. The idea for a new university in the St. Louis area had its start in the 1840's when some of the leading citizens of the day became concerned about the lack of institutions of higher learning in the Midwest. The university is unique amongst large, exclusive centers of learning in that there was no large financial endowment used to create the university. Funding for the operations of the university initially came through tuition and some local support from wealthy citizens. The university has students from all 50 U.S. states and from 120 countries around the world. Twenty-two Nobel laureates have been a part of Washington University over the past century. Nine of those Nobel winners conducted their primary research on the campus.

The 1904 Summer Olympics

In 1904, the Summer Olympics were hosted by the city of St. Louis. These games are officially known as the Games of the III Olympiad. Many of the events for the Olympics were held on the grounds of Washington University in an area that now houses Francis Field. It was the first time in history that the Olympics were held outside Europe. Chicago, IL originally won the rights to host the 1904 Summer Olympics. When the organizers of the St. Louis Fair won their bid to host the Louisiana Purchase Exposition for that same year they began to negotiate to move the games from Chicago to St. Louis. The negotiations became so intense that the World's Fair organizers threatened to plan their own sporting event that they said would eclipse the Olympic Games. It took the efforts of Pierre de Coubertin, the founder of the modern Olympic games, to get Chicago to give in and transfer the games to St. Louis.

Many of the top athletes from around the world were unable to attend the Olympic Games. Political tensions in Europe caused by the Russo-Japanese War kept many athletes away. The St. Louis Olympics did have athletes from over 13 countries and featured 15 different sport competitions. Boxing, freestyle wrestling, and the decathlon made their debuts at these Olympic games.

One of the most remarkable athletes was an American gymnast who won six medals at the games. George Eyser competed in all the gymnastic events and was a crowd favorite. His medal winnings were remarkable because he had a wooded left leg.

The most bizarre event of the St. Louis Olympic games is undoubtedly the running of the marathon. To begin with, the weather was brutally hot. The marathon was run on roads so dusty that spectators had trouble seeing the runners. Then there was a question as to which marathoner was the first to cross the finish line. It was assumed that Frederick Lorz arrived first and the awards ceremony was about to begin. But, it was quickly found out that Lorz dropped out after only nine miles. He was picked up by an automobile that was taking him back to the finish line when the car broke down at the 19th mile. Lorz decided to re-enter the race and jogged to the finish line. Fortunately, before the medal was awarded, his deception was found out and the awards ceremony was delayed as they awaited the true finishers to cross the finish line.

Thomas Hicks, a Briton running for the United States, was the first to cross the finish line – legally. Hicks had dosed himself with strychnine, a common rat poison, and swallowed a shot of brandy prior to the start of the race. His trainers thought this would stimulate his nervous system and allow him to finish the race in record time. Just after crossing the finish line, Hicks went into convulsions and nearly died. Fortunately, doctors in the stadiums were able to treat him and he survived.

Felix Carbajal arrived from Cuba just minutes before the race gun sounded. He had no time to change into his running clothes, so he started the race in his street clothes. He quickly tore off his pant legs to make them look like shorts. Along the marathon route, Felix got hungry and paused by an apple orchard to enjoy some apples. Unfortunately, the apples were rotten. Between the long journey from Cuba and the rotten apples, Felix got tired and decided to lie down and take a nap. Despite his little rest alongside the marathon route, Felix still ended up taking fourth place.

The first black Africans to compete in the Olympic games also ran the marathon in the St. Louis Olympics. Len Taunyane and Jan Mashiani were Tswana tribesman and part of a sideshow sponsored by the South African government at the 1904 World's Fair. Taunyane finished ninth and Mashiani, twelfth. There was some disappointment that Taunyane did not finish higher, but he had been chased nearly a mile off course by aggressive dogs.

St. Louis, MO – Forest Park and Central West End

> **Turn Right at Lindell Blvd, crossing Skinker Blvd**
> **After crossing Skinker Blvd, continue on the Forest Park walking trail with Lindell Blvd. on your left.**
> **Take a quick break as you walk along this trail for Stop 12.**

Stop 12:
Lindell Blvd Mansions and Old Route 66 (Lindell Blvd.)

As you walk along this portion of the trail in Forest Park, glance over to your left. You are seeing more than just Lindell Blvd. The road that you see is also part of one of the most extraordinary roads ever developed in the United States. This portion of Lindell Blvd. is one of the remaining segments of Route 66 left in the St. Louis area. Route 66, "The Will Rogers Highway," or "The Mother Road," started in 1927. The route, from Chicago, IL across to Santa Monica, CA, was one of the most magical roads in the entire world. Noted architect Frank Lloyd Wright once remarked, "Route 66 is a giant chute down which everything loose in this country is sliding into southern California."

Looking beyond old Route 66 you see some of the many fine mansions that were built by the leaders of business in the St. Louis area in the late 19th century. The development of Washington University and the 1904 World's Fair helped turned the area you see into prime real estate land. Unique and restrictive covenants were enacted to ensure that the homes were large and would be maintained in almost palatial status for decades.

The history of the suburbs of St. Louis is significant. So is the development of private roads. In the late 1860's, city planner Julius Pitzman conceived the idea of private streets to control real estate speculation and to maintain property standards. This was in an era before zoning laws offered such protections. A private street, such as those you see across Lindell Blvd., is a self-governing enclave with common areas owned by residents. Services, such as trash pickup and lawn care, are provided by the private sector. City resources are rarely used, or needed. These privately controlled single-family home communities operate very similar to condominiums or homeowners associations that we are familiar with today.

Private streets have the ability to control the traffic in these exclusive neighborhoods. Many of the streets are gated at the ends to prevent traffic from using the streets as thoroughfares. There is a quiet, almost park-like atmosphere as you walk through these neighborhoods. The City of St. Louis does provide police and fire protection, but all other services and the maintenance of such things as sidewalks, planting trees, even paving of the streets, is paid for by the homeowners on each street. In just a little while, this walk will take you through even more of these exclusive home areas in the Central West End district.

St. Louis, MO – Forest Park and Central West End

> - Continue on the walking trail admiring the beautiful homes along Lindell Blvd. on your left.
> - After passing the Missouri History Museum on your RIGHT, turn RIGHT on to the walking trail at the second stoplight.
> - Follow the sidewalk as it takes you to the Forest Park Visitor Center.
> - This would be a good time to take a break before continuing on with your Wandering Walk.
> - After your break, go to the front of the Visitor Center and walk straight on the sidewalk crossing Grand Dr.
> - Continue on sidewalk as it crosses Theater Circle and walk to Stop 13.

Stop 13:
Pagoda Circle Bandstand
(Forest Park)

As you walk across Theater Circle and head towards the Muny Theater, you will see an island in the center of Pagoda Lake. This was the site of Forest Park's first bandstand which dates back to the Park's origins in 1876. The original pagoda-shaped bandstand was used until 1911, when it was deemed unsafe after a severe storm nearly destroyed it. In 1924, Nathan Frank donated a new bandstand to the park. The more classically-styled bandstand provides small concerts and is the site for many weddings.

> Continue straight ahead on the sidewalk to Stop 14.

Stop 14: Municipal Theater (The Muny) (1 Theater Dr.)

The Municipal Theater, commonly called The Muny, has operated in Forest Park since 1916. The first production was *As You Like It* by William Shakespeare. This production took place on a small grassy area between two giant oak trees near today's current site. In 1919, the 11,000-seat outdoor amphitheater was built. The first show in this new amphitheater was a production of *Robin Hood*. The production was notable because the popular mayor of St. Louis at the time, Henry Kiel, played the part of King Richard. Since it's opening, the last nine rows of seats, approximately 1,500 seats, are free and available on a first come, first served basis.

The Muny is the nation's oldest and largest outdoor musical theater. There is no lawn seating and most shows are sold out months in advance. Due to its size, many of the best and biggest Broadway-style musical shows are performed in the theater throughout the summer. Thousands of performers have performed at The Muny in its nearly 100 years of providing quality theater experiences for the young and old alike.

> In front of the Muny Theater turn right.
> Turn Left at McKinley Dr and continue on sidewalk walking up the hill.
> At the top of the hill, cross Wells Drive and walk to the entrance of Stop 15.

Stop 15:
The Jewel Box
(5600 Clayton Ave.)

The Jewel Box is the home of the St. Louis Floral Conservatory. It is one of the most beautiful buildings on the grounds of Forest Park. This large greenhouse was designed by William Becker. Work was completed on the building in 1936. The greenhouse was built during a time of extreme smoke and soot in the city caused by the thousands of manufacturing plants. The greenhouse was a way to save certain plants that were dying because of the air pollution and preserve them for future generations. It is said that when the greenhouse opened someone said the displays "looked like a jewel box." And that is where the name of the greenhouse originated.

Due to large hailstorms in the Midwest, the roof is not composed of glass, but rather, large wooden planks. There are over 4,000 plate glass windows surrounding the walls of the Jewel box.

- ➢ With your back to the front entrance of the Jewell Box, turn left on sidewalk.
- ➢ Left at next sidewalk.
- ➢ Right on walking trail just before Union Dr.
- ➢ Continue straight on Wells Dr. as trail ends and walk downhill with baseball diamonds on your left.
- ➢ Cross Jefferson Dr. and continue straight on the gravel walking trail.
- ➢ At next "Y" intersection on the trail, turn left on the gravel walking trail.
- ➢ Just before the bridge on the trail, turn right on the gravel trail.
- ➢ Continue to Stop 16.

Stop 16: Victorian Footbridge (Forest Park)

As your walk takes you away from Forest Park, you will cross over an ornate truss bridge. This suspension-like pedestrian bridge was built in 1885 as a crossing over the River des Peres. It continues to be a beautiful link between Forest Park and the Central West End district of St. Louis.

St. Louis, MO – Forest Park and Central West End

> After walking across the Victorian Footbridge, continue straight on the walking trail.
> Walk up the stairs and cross over two more pedestrian bridges on the trail.
> Turn Right when the sidewalk ends (West Pine Dr.) and walk towards the light at Kingshighway.
> Pause here to read about the Central West End Neighborhood you are about to enter.

Stop 17:
Central West End Neighborhood (Kingshighway Blvd.)

You are about to enter one of the most historic neighborhoods in St. Louis, the Central West End. It's difficult to imagine today as you see large skyscrapers, multi-lane roads, and thousands of cars, but when Forest Park was created in 1876, this was rolling farmland. It didn't take long after the Park's dedication for the wealthier citizens of St. Louis to realize this would be a perfect spot to build homes and escape the confines and noise of the growing city.

To add a measure of privacy and security for the large mansions being developed in this area, a new concept called "private places" was created. As no zoning laws existed in St. Louis at the turn of the 20th century, homeowners created covenants and strict regulations regarding building standards. Street maintenance, front gardens, and small greenspaces along the streets, created a near park-like atmosphere. Today, these private streets and outstanding turn-of-the-century homes retain the beauty and peace envisioned over 125 years ago.

Over the years, the Central West End has been home to many famous people in both art and business. Playwright Tennessee Williams lived on Westminster Place. The rear fire escape on his home undoubtedly inspired the opening scene of *The Glass Menagerie*. Author Kate Chopin, whom many consider to be one of the earliest feminist writers, lived on McPherson Avenue. Poet T.S. Eliot lived for a while in this historic neighborhood.

Some noted business leaders at the turn of the 20th century made the Central West End their home. Albert Lambert, a pioneering pilot and largest benefactor of Charles Lindbergh's historic solo flight to Paris lived in the neighborhood. Ralston Purina, founder of the largest pet food company in the world, lived on Kingsbury Place. Newspaper publisher Joseph Pulitzer constructed a large mansion on Pershing Place. Dwight Davis, founder of the Davis Cup Tennis Tournament lived on Portland Place.

During the Great Depression and the slow-down in business following the end of World War II, the Central West End saw a decline in home ownership. Many homes and buildings were left standing vacant. As the highway system improved during the 1960's, large numbers of families moved from the area to even larger homes in the suburbs of St. Louis.

Since the late 1990's, the area has seen a dramatic revitalization. Homes are being renovated and rebuilt back to their former. Trendy new restaurants and shopping boutiques are popping up on Euclid Ave. Residents are returning as the Central West End is now one of the most sought after places to live in the city.

> **Cross Kingshighway and continue straight on West Pine Blvd to Stop 18.**

Stop 18:
Forest Park Hotel
(4910 West Pine Blvd.)

The six-story Forest Park Hotel was built in 1923. It is one of hundreds of buildings and homes listed on the National Register of Historic Places in the Central West End neighborhood. The original hotel was designed by Preston Bradshaw, a noted St. Louis architect, who also designed the nearby Chase Park Plaza Hotel and the five-star Mayfair Hotel in downtown St. Louis.

One of the most famous nightclubs in the St. Louis area during the 1930's and 1940's, was the Circus Snack Bar Nightclub, located on the ground floor of the Forest Park Hotel. Liberace and Louis Armstrong were just some of the more famous performers to entertain the guests of the Circus Snack Bar.

In 2003, the hotel was closed and converted into an apartment complex.

> Continue on West Pine Blvd. to Stop 19.

Stop 19: Butler House (4484 West Pine Blvd.)

This turreted, brick house is one of the oldest homes in the Central West End. St. Louis tobacco manufacturer James Butler had his home built in the Queen Anne style in 1892. The ornamental detailing on the house's exterior makes it stand out from all the other houses on the block.

James Butler made his wealth in the tobacco business and was the director and major shareholder of the American Tobacco Company. In 1912, Butler became the founder of the Bank of St. Louis. A bank that would become the largest and most prominent in the city. Prior to his rise in the business world, Butler fought in the American Civil War on the side of the Union. He earned the rank of Major after fighting in Tennessee, Missouri, and Arkansas.

> **Continue on West Pine Blvd.**
> **Right on Newstead Ave. to Stop 30**

Stop 20:
Cathedral Basilica of St. Louis
(4431 Lindell Blvd.)

The Cathedral Basilica of Saint Louis was completed in 1914. It is the mother church of the Roman Catholic Archdiocese of St. Louis and the seat of its archbishop. The cathedral is named for Saint Louis and was designated a basilica by Pope John Paul II in 1997.

This is not the first, nor only, Cathedral in St. Louis. The first cathedral, which still exists, is located on the banks of the Mississippi River. Today that much smaller cathedral sits directly below the shadow of the Gateway Arch. By the late 1800's, the Archbishop of St. Louis determined that the smaller cathedral in downtown St. Louis needed a new building and location. The population in the downtown area was beginning to decline and the growth of new homes was occurring west of the city in the area we know of today as the Central West End.

In 1907 a groundbreaking ceremony was held to begin clearing the site for the new cathedral. It took over seven years for the building to be constructed. The dedication and first mass took place on October 18, 1914. Consecration of the cathedral took place more than a decade later in 1926.

While the outside of the cathedral is a marvel to admire, it's when you inside that you see the true wonder of this magnificent place of worship.

The church is famous for its large mosaics, which are the largest in the Western Hemisphere. In 1912, the mosaic work began. It took until 1988 for the 41.5 million pieces of glass tesserae, using more than 7,000 different colors, to be installed. In total, the mosaics cover over 80,000 square feet of interior space. Many of the mosaics were designed by the Tiffany Studios of New York and directed by Louis Comfort Tiffany. Throughout the interior of the building you can find mosaics that depict the life of King Louis IX of France, significant archdiocesan events, and Biblical scenes from both the Old and New Testaments. With so much to see, the church has created a brochure called "A Quest Among the Mosaics of the Cathedral Basilica of Saint Louis." This informative brochure points out many of the religious and historic events depicted on the walls and ceiling of the cathedral.

The church basement contains a museum dedicated to the mosaics in the church. The basement contains other important artifacts associated with the cathedral and the Roman Catholic Archdiocese in the St. Louis area. The crypts of former Archbishops are also located in the basement area.

> **Continue on Newstead Ave.**
> **Left on Westminster Place.**
> **As you walk along Westminster Place, read about its history at stop 21.**

Stop 21: Fullerton's Westminster Place (Westminster Place)

This private street district in the Central West End was created by Joseph Fullerton, a Civil War general. In 1882, the 4300 and 4400 blocks of Westminster Place began its initial construction of large homes.

Using the new real estate development technique knowns as a "private place," the houses were required to follow more stringent requirements and protections than normal zoning laws provided. This included having the homes setback further from the street, a minimum cost for the construction of the home, and the style of home that could be erected. The result was having homes built on private streets that offer the park-like atmosphere you see today. Most of the homes you see along this street are in the Georgian, Romanesque, and Renaissance Revival styles popular at the turn of the 20th century.

> **Continue on Westminster Place.**
> **Cross Taylor St and pause for Stop 22.**

Stop 22:
Second Presbyterian Church
(4501 Westminster Place)

The chapel portion of the Second Presbyterian Church was constructed in 1896 in the Romanesque Revival style. Henry Richardson was the original designer of the church. Richardson is most famous for designing the famous Trinity Church in Boston.

In 1899, the sanctuary portion of the church was built using the same Romanesque Revival style. This time, the construction was led by a local architect, Theodore Link. Link is most well known as the designer of the St. Louis Union Station.

St. Louis, MO – Forest Park and Central West End

> ➤ Continue on Westminster Place.
> ➤ Left on Euclid.
> ➤ Right on Hortense Place.
> ➤ Cross Kingshighway and continue on Waterman Blvd. to Stop 23.

Stop 23:
Joseph Erlanger House
(5127 Waterman Blvd)

The homes in the Central West End are beautiful and lovingly maintained. Walking through the neighborhoods and along the private streets is like walking through a park. That is why a well-known doctor and physiologist chose to live in this area. Joseph Erlanger moved into this home on Waterman Blvd. in 1917. Dr. Erlanger was a professor and researcher at Washington University. In 1944, Dr. Erlanger, along with his research partner, Herbert Gasser, won the Nobel Prize for Medicine. They identified several varieties of nerve fiber and documented the relationship between velocity and fiber diameter that would have major implications in the development of the treatment of brain disorders and pharmaceuticals to slow seizures in patients.

> Continue on Waterman Blvd.
> Left on Union St.
> Cross Lindell Blvd to re-enter Forest Park.
> Right on Grand Dr. and continue on gravel trail back to the Forest Park Visitor Center and your vehicle.

3

OTHER SITES TO VISIT IN THE REGION

The Gateway Arch and the Jefferson National Expansion Memorial.
707 N. 1st St. • St. Louis, MO

Discover magnificent views 630-feet in the sky from the top of St. Louis' Gateway Arch—an iconic monument symbolizing the city's role as early settlers pioneered westward years ago. Learn about the history and culture surrounding the city in the Museum of Westward Expansion at the base of the Arch. Both the Arch and the museum are part of the Jefferson National Expansion Memorial run by the National Park Service.

First Missouri State Capital State Historic Site
200 S. Main St • St. Charles, MO

From 1821 to 1826, the state capital of Missouri was in St. Charles, MO. A visit to this state historic site allows you to see the fully restored legislative chambers, while a visit to the interpretive center offers exhibits on the early history of the state of Missouri.

Anheuser-Busch Brewery Tours
12th and Lynch Sts. • St. Louis, MO

Tours include the historic brew house, the Budweiser Clydesdale stable, the beechwood aging cellar, and the packaging plant. At the end of the tour, those over the age of 21 are welcome to test drive a freshly brewed beer of their choice.

Ulysses S. Grant National Historic Site (White Haven Home)
7400 Grant Rd • St. Louis, MO

For many years, Ulysses S. Grant lived in a home that belonged to the family of his wife, Julia. Tours of the home are given daily. Here you learn that the man who defeated the Confederacy had once lived on a farm where slaves were kept.

Grant's Farm
10501 Gravois Rd • St. Louis, MO

This Busch family estate was once owned by Ulysses S. Grant. Today, there are animal shows, petting zoos, and a train ride through a wildlife preserve.

Jefferson Barracks Historic Park and National Cemetery
533 Grant Rd • St. Louis, MO

Jefferson Barracks was once one of the largest military camps west of the Mississippi River. Robert E. Lee and Ulysses S. Grant both served on this military base. In 1866, a national cemetery was created on the grounds. Military personnel from the War of Independence through the present day are interred within the cemetery.

Route 66 Sidewalk Plaques
7200-7400 Manchester Rd • Maplewood, MO

Maplewood, MO pays tribute to iconic Route 66. Walking the "Mother Road" along Manchester Rd. takes visitors down memory lane. Unique sidewalk plaques and murals enhance your walk.

The Magic House, St. Louis Children's Museum
516 S. Kirkwood Rd. • St. Louis, MO

This nationally acclaimed children's museum offers hundreds of hands-on activities and fun, educational things for kids to do on a daily basis.

Six Flags St. Louis
I-44 Southwest of St. Louis • Eureka, MO

Looking for fun, excitement, and maybe a heart-stopping ride on some of the wildest rollercoasters in the nation, then Six Flags is just the place to visit. Hurricane Harbor, a 12-acre water park, is also included with the price of admission.

Ted Drewes Frozen Custard
Old Rte 66, 6726 Chippewa • St. Louis, MO

While much of old Route 66 is gone throughout the St. Louis area, one place has stayed the same. Ted Drewes has been a St. Louis tradition on Old Route 66 since 1929. Their frozen custard is so thick you can turn the cup upside down and not lose a drop.

Tower Grove Park
4256 Magnolia Ave • St. Louis, MO

This 289-acre National Historic Landmark park offers a quiet oasis in the middle of the city. Walking trails, birdwatching, and small festivals surround the Victorian-era pavilions. It's a great place to relax and unwind after a day of walking and sightseeing.

Cahokia Mounds State Historic Site
30 Ramey St. • Collinsville, IL

Just across the Missouri River, is the site of the largest prehistoric Indian city complexes and burial mounds north of Mexico. A visit to this site allows you to see the mounds up close. The visitor center offers exhibits on the original inhabitants of this region.

A Wandering Walk Guide Book

If you enjoyed this guidebook, we have many more to choose from. Got to www.wanderingwalksofwonder.com for more books and journals..

Walking Guidebook:
St. Louis, MO- Downtown

Walking Guidebook:
Hannibal, MO

Walking Guidebook:
Independence, MO

My Road Trip
Journal

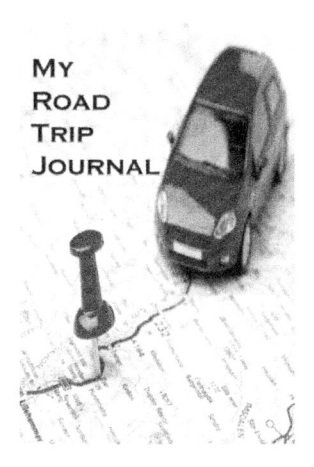

ABOUT THE AUTHOR

The author, Tom Alyea, is an avid walker, hiker and author of numerous books, guidebooks, and journals. He spends most of his time walking across the United States and around the world finding ways that he can rediscover a new life on the trail and motivate others to do the same.

Tom is also a member of the only national walking club in the U.S. – The American Volkssport Association.

Made in the USA
Monee, IL
20 June 2023